W9-CGT-217

ON THE HUNT WITH KOMODO DRAGONS

BY KRISTEN POPE

The Child's World®

childsworld.com

Published by The Child's World®
1980 Lookout Drive • Mankato, MN 56003-1705
800-599-READ • www.childsworld.com

Acknowledgments
The Child's World®: Mary Berendes, Publishing Director
Red Line Editorial: Design, editorial direction, and production
Photographs ©: Richard Susanto/Shutterstock Images, cover, 1; Goddard
Photography/iStockphoto, 4; Shutterstock Images, 6, 13; Kirsten Wahlquist/
Shutterstock Images, 7; Anna Yu/iStockphoto, 9; Tepikina Nastya/
Shutterstock Images, 10; Red Line Editorial, 12; iStockphoto, 14; Gudkov
Andrey/Shutterstock Images, 16; Sergey Uryadnikov/Shutterstock Images, 17;
Tui De Roy/Minden Pictures/Corbis, 18; Phil Noble/Reuters/Corbis, 20; Kjersti
Joergensen/Shutterstock Images, 21

ISBN 9781634074544

LCCN 2015946264

Printed in the United States of America
Mankato, MN
December, 2015
PA02279

TABLE OF
CONTENTS

Chapter 1

ON THE HUNT

A powerful Komodo dragon sits in the grass. It hides next to a **game trail**. The large lizard smells something in the distance. The Komodo dragon flicks its long, yellow, forked tongue. The breeze is blowing a very slight scent its way.

After flicking its tongue, the Komodo dragon pulls its tongue into its mouth. It touches its tongue softly to the roof of its mouth. It has an organ there called a **Jacobson's organ**. This organ lets the Komodo dragon know food is nearby. The left fork of its tongue has a stronger scent on it. This means the **prey** is coming from the left. The prey might not get to the lizard for a while, though. Komodo dragons can detect their prey from more than 1 mile (1.6 km) away.

As the lizard waits, scars shine on its yellowish gray back. Its rough skin is covered with scars. These old wounds are from a battle with a wild boar. Fights are not always easy. That is why the Komodo dragon must be ready to defend itself.

◄ **Komodo dragons use their tongues to smell and find prey.**

▲ Komodo dragons' rough, scaly skin is very tough.

In the distance, the Komodo dragon sees tall grass waving slightly. The prey is coming this way. The animal is a Timor deer. It is almost a distance of three football fields away. But the Komodo dragon can see it well.

The deer comes closer. The Komodo dragon gets ready to attack. The lizard makes sure its 150-pound (68-kg), 8-foot-(2.4-m) long body is hidden in the tall grass. Komodo dragons are the largest lizards alive in the world today. Then, when the deer is only a few feet away, the dragon attacks. With a snap of its jaw, the Komodo dragon sinks its teeth into the deer's leg. The deer squeals. The Komodo dragon digs its long claws into the deer's flesh. The dragon tries hard to hold the deer down.

Struggling to get away, the deer tries with all its might to escape. The deer kicks the Komodo dragon in the mouth. One of

▲ Komodo dragons have long, sharp claws.

the Komodo dragon's teeth flies out and lands in the grass. The tooth is short and sharp. The lizard is okay, though. The Komodo dragon has 60 short, sharp teeth in its mouth. A new one will grow in the old tooth's place. A single Komodo might go through four or five sets of teeth in its lifetime.

Using its claws, the Komodo dragon gets in one more swipe at the deer. The deer jumps up and limps away. The Komodo dragon doesn't follow. It knows that the deer will likely die from its wounds within 24 hours. The dragon will have its meal soon. It just has to be patient. The 50 strains of bacteria in the Komodo dragon's mouth are doing their work. The deer will soon get an infection and become very weak.

Komodo dragon teeth are very small and short. ▶

Chapter 2

RESTING IN SHADE

The midday sun beats down. It is hotter than 95° Fahrenheit (35°C) and is very humid. Islands in Indonesia are usually very hot. Komodo dragons live only on five islands in Indonesia. It is time for the Komodo dragon to relax. A shady tree sits a few feet to the dragon's left. Underneath the tree, the dragon rests in the shade.

There is one place even cooler than the tree's shade: the dragon's **burrow**. The Komodo dragon walks back toward its burrow. Its home is not far away. The burrow is in a dry streambed. Ducking under tree roots, the dragon slips inside. The temperature is much lower inside. The burrow is nice and cool. It is a perfect place to rest. And at night, the burrow is warm.

Later, the Komodo dragon comes out of its burrow. The lizard is cooler now. It flicks its tongue in and out. It touches its Jacobson's organ. The dragon can smell that the deer is nearby again. It can also smell that the deer is dying. Soon, the Komodo

◄ **Komodo dragons escape hot temperatures by resting in shady areas.**

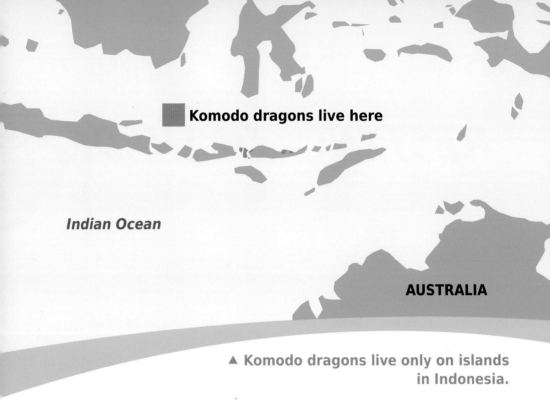

Komodo dragons live here

Indian Ocean

AUSTRALIA

▲ Komodo dragons live only on islands in Indonesia.

dragon will have its meal. The organ doesn't just tell the Komodo dragon about prey nearby. The scent organ also helps it know if other Komodo dragons are in the area.

Another Komodo dragon is out at sea. It is swimming. The dragon is coming from another island. Its powerful tail helps it swim through the rough seas. It is here for a meal. Many Komodo dragons share a single kill. The Komodo dragon steps out of the water and walks up on the beach.

Both dragons smell the dying deer. Then they see movement. The deer is limping. It looks very sick. It goes into the bushes. Now the Komodo dragons will finish off the deer. Using its short, powerful legs, one Komodo runs toward its prey.

With its sharp teeth and powerful claws, one of the dragons takes the deer down. Now the dragons will eat. Using their flat, long heads with mouths full of sharp teeth, they grab hunks of meat. Komodo dragons can eat massive amounts of meat in one meal. The 150-pound (68-kg) Komodo dragon can eat up to 120 pounds (54 kg) of meat in one meal. In less than one minute, it can eat 5 pounds (2 kg) of meat.

▲ **Komodo dragons can run up to 13 miles (21 km) per hour over short distances.**

Chapter 3

PART OF THE GROUP

As the two Komodo dragons eat, a younger Komodo dragon watches from high up in a nearby tree. After a few minutes, there is hardly anything left of the deer. The other dragons ate almost all of it. The small Komodo dragon carefully walks up near the group. It hopes to get some leftovers from their meal. But the young dragon is careful. Sometimes, adult males will kill young Komodo dragons.

One of the large males hisses at the newcomer. The young Komodo dragon steps back. The older one lunges. It nicks the younger one with its teeth. The young dragon decides to leave—and fast! The young one turns around and races back up the tree. The large Komodo dragon will not follow. It is too big to climb trees. The young one has a small wound. It does not have to worry

◀ Smaller Komodo dragons find protection in trees.

▲ Before fighting, adult Komodo dragons puff out their throats and thrash their tails.

about infection, though. The bacteria in a Komodo dragon's mouth is not dangerous to other Komodo dragons.

After eating all that meat from the deer, the Komodo dragons will not need to eat again anytime soon. They can go for weeks without another meal. A Komodo dragon can survive on just 1 pound (.5 kg) of food per day. And there is no need for them to find water today. They do not need much water. They can get most of the water they need through the meat they eat. This is helpful because sometimes the islands go long periods of time without rain.

There isn't much left of the deer now. Some of the larger dragons are already lying in the shade. As they lie down, the

Komodo dragons see more movement. A water buffalo is moving far away. The dragons are full now and won't go after the buffalo. The squeal of a wild pig breaks the still air. The sound is coming from very far away. Another Komodo dragon must have found a meal of its own.

Komodo dragons will eat almost any kind of meat. Sometimes they will eat snakes. Other times they will eat fish that wash up on the beach. Komodo dragons will attack live prey and also eat dead animal flesh. They are top **predators**. This means they are at the top of the food chain.

The Komodo dragons now all lie in the shade. They control their body temperature by moving between the shade and the sun. They do not use much energy.

▲ **Older Komodo dragons rest on the ground while the youngest rest in the trees.**

Chapter 4

HIDDEN EGGS

A Komodo dragon nest is only a short distance away from the resting lizards. Inside the nest, one of the eggs is wiggling. It is smooth, 2 inches (5 cm) wide, and 4 inches (10 cm) long. This **clutch**, or group of eggs, has 25 eggs. The mother Komodo dragon dug this hole as a nest for her babies.

The real nest is dug next to a fake nest. The fake nest is dug to trick predators. Sometimes other animals want to eat Komodo dragon eggs. Sometimes adult Komodo males will eat the eggs, too. The fake nest is a way to trick these predators and keep them from finding the real eggs.

Soon, a baby Komodo dragon hatches. The baby is brown, yellow, and orange. It has a few black and white spots and stripes. The different colors help it blend in with its surroundings. After it hatches, the baby scampers away. It runs up a tree. It already knows that it is not safe.

◄ **A mother Komodo dragon protects her nest, which is a small burrow in a sandy hillside.**

▲ Komodo dragon babies are just
1 foot (0.3 m) long when they are born.

The new dragon stays up in the tree. It eats grasshoppers, beetles, geckos, and eggs it finds in trees. The baby dragon likes hollow tree trunks because geckos hide in them. Geckos are its favorite food.

When a Komodo dragon is about four years old, it will be about 4 feet (1 m) long. Then it is too big to climb trees. It starts living on the ground. At that age, the dragon does not have to worry about other adult Komodo dragons eating it. The adults are not as likely to eat it because it is bigger.

When Komodo dragons are about eight years old, they are fully grown. By this time, the dragon is a top predator on the island. Its big, muscular tail can be as long as the rest of its body. But until then, the baby Komodo dragon has to stay in the tree. The little dragon has a lot of growing up to do before it is a top predator on the island.

▲ Komodo dragons live in trees for the first four years of their lives, blending into the trees for protection.

GLOSSARY

bacteria (bak-TEER-ee-uh): Bacteria are single-celled living things that can sometimes be harmful. The bacteria in the Komodo dragon's mouth infects its prey.

burrow (BUR-oh): A burrow is a tunnel or hole that an animal uses as a home. On hot days, the Komodo dragon rests in its cool, shaded burrow.

clutch (kluhch): A clutch is a group of eggs laid by an animal, usually in a nest. The clutch of eggs was hidden in a burrow.

game trail (game trayl): A game trail is a route that animals use. The Komodo dragon hid by the game trail, waiting for its prey to walk by.

Jacobson's organ (JAKUB-suns OR-guhn): A Jacobson's organ is a scent organ on the roof of an animal's mouth. A Komodo dragon flicks its tongue and places it on its Jacobson's organ to sense what is nearby.

predators (PRED-uh-turs): Predators are animals that eat other animals. Komodo dragons are large, fierce predators.

prey (PRAY): Prey are animals that are eaten by other animals. Deer are the prey of Komodo dragons.

TO LEARN MORE

Books

Meister, Cari. *Komodo Dragons*. Minneapolis, MN: Jump!, 2016.

Raum, Elizabeth. *Komodo Dragons*. Mankato, MN: Amicus High Interest, 2015.

Turnbull, Stephanie. *Komodo Dragon*. Mankato, MN: Smart Apple Media, 2015.

Web Sites

Visit our Web site for links about Komodo dragons:
childsworld.com/links

Note to Parents, Teachers, and Librarians: We routinely verify our Web links to make sure they are safe and active sites. So encourage your readers to check them out!

SELECTED BIBLIOGRAPHY

"Komodo Dragon." *National Geographic*. National Geographic, n.d. Web. 4 June 2015.

"Komodo Dragon." *San Diego Zoo Animals*. San Diego Zoo Global, 2015. Web. 9 June 2015.

"Komodo Dragon." *Smithsonian National Zoological Park*. Smithsonian National Zoological Park, n.d. Web. 10 June 2015.

"Komodo Dragon." *Woodland Park Zoo*. Woodland Park Zoo, 2015. Web. 6 June 2015.

INDEX

ABOUT THE AUTHOR

Kristen Pope is a writer and editor with years of experience working in national and state parks and museums. She has a master's degree in natural resources and has taught people of all ages about science and the environment. She has even coaxed reluctant insect-lovers to pet Madagascar hissing cockroaches.